COMPOSER SHOWCASE
HAL LEONARD STUDENT PIANO LIBRARY

Jazz Starters III

ORIGINAL PIANO SOLOS IN VARIOUS JAZZ STYLES

BY BILL BOYD

CONTENTS

Editor: Barbara Kreader

ISBN 0-7935-3464-X

HAL•LEONARD® CORPORATION

7777 W. BLUEMOUND RD. P.O. BOX 13819 MILWAUKEE, WI 53213

Visit Hal Leonard Online at
www.halleonard.com

INTRODUCTION

The compositions in this book are written in several jazz styles and are well-suited for students who are comfortable playing hands together, moving to various five-finger positions on the keyboard, and reading rhythms in eighth notes.

Too Blue creates a "bluesy" feeling because the melody emphasizes the flatted third (E-Flat in the key of this piece) and flatted seventh (B-Flat), the so-called blues notes.

Boogie Rock and *Woogie Boogie* are two examples of the boogie-woogie style.

The melodies of *Minor Blue* and *Hickory Dickory Rock* are based on the notes of the minor blues scale. Jazz musicians often use this scale when they improvise.

The left-hand dotted-quarter and eighth-note rhythm in *Too Cool To Fool* suggests the bass parts played by the bass guitar or acoustic bass in rock pieces.

A different kind of ragtime sound is heard in *Ragtime Waltz*.

Two-Four-Six-Eight exhibits a typical swing blues sound. It is written in 6/8 time and prepares students for "swing," or unevenly played eighths.

Imagine a Dixieland band playing a song that features the tuba (in this case the left hand) and you will understand the style of *The Dixieland Tuba*.

Igneous Rock, a rock piece in a minor key, offers a chance to play rock chords in both hands.

The left-hand bass pattern in *Back Porch Swing* is typical of swing-style jazz.

In *Jazz Theme And Variation* a jazz melody is simply stated and then repeated with a different accompaniment or improvisation.

TOO BLUE

By Bill Boyd

Slowly

BOOGIE ROCK

By Bill Boyd

MINOR BLUE

By Bill Boyd

Moderately

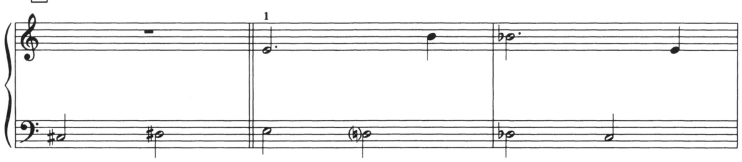

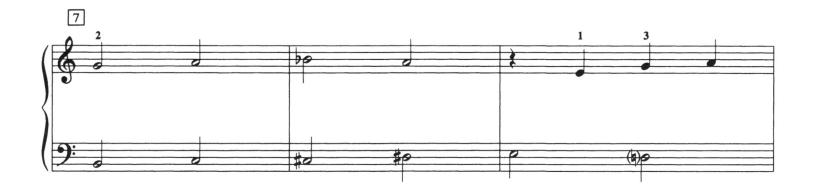

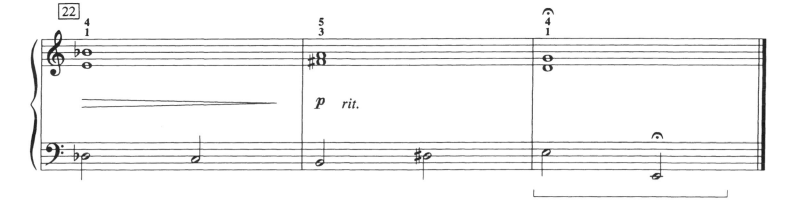

TOO COOL TO FOOL

By Bill Boyd

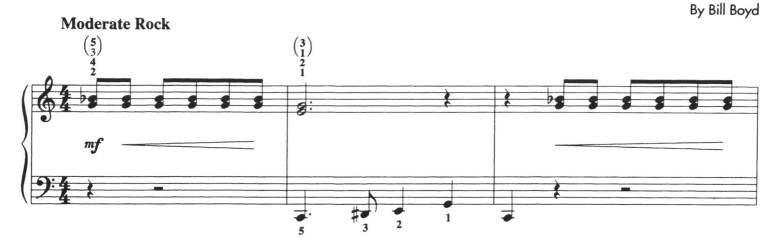

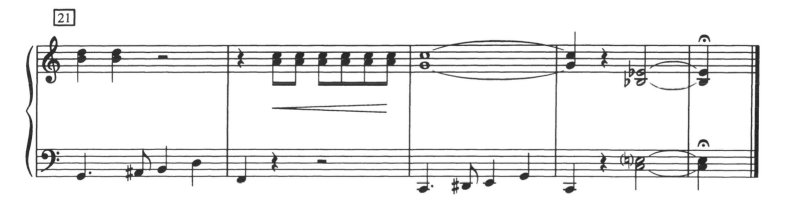

RAGTIME WALTZ

By Bill Boyd

Moderately

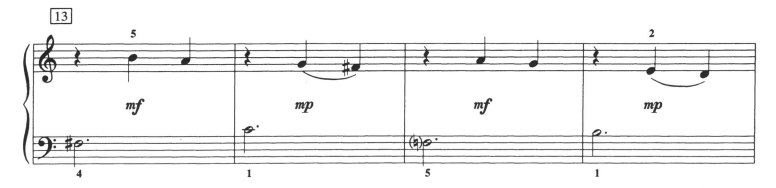

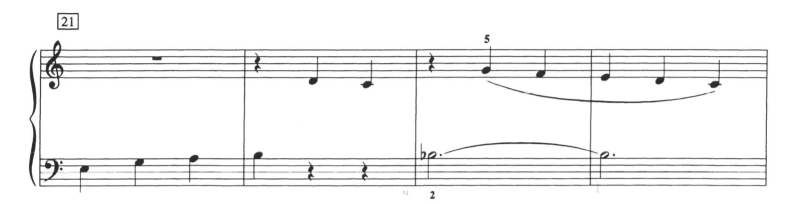

TWO - FOUR - SIX - EIGHT

By Bill Boyd

Quickly (In 6)

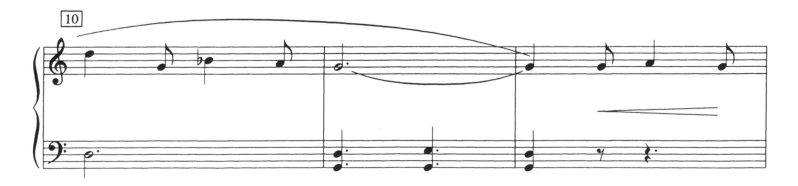

12

HICKORY DICKORY ROCK

By Bill Boyd

Moderately fast Rock

THE DIXIELAND TUBA

By Bill Boyd

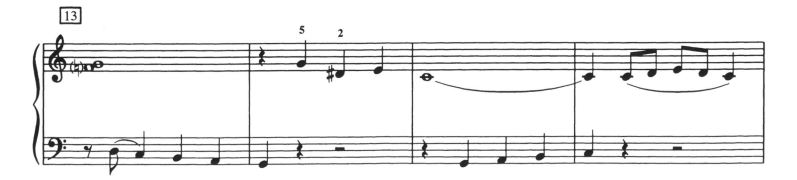

IGNEOUS ROCK

By Bill Boyd

Moderately fast

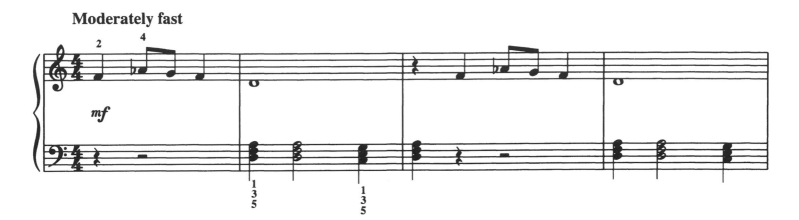

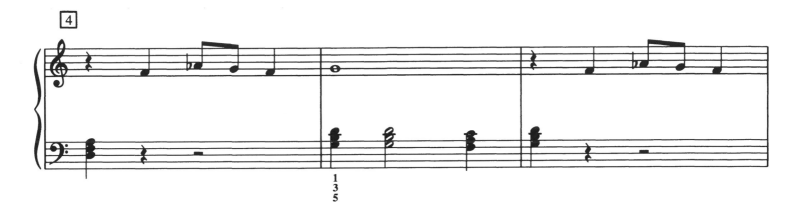

Bring out L.H. melody

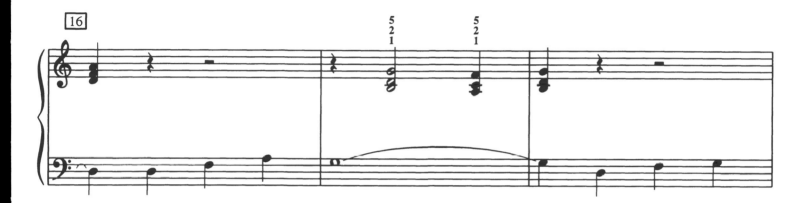

WOOGIE BOOGIE

By Bill Boyd

BACK PORCH SWING

By Bill Boyd

Moderate Swing

Play R.H. one octave higher 2nd time

loco

JAZZ THEME AND VARIATION

By Bill Boyd

Moderately slow

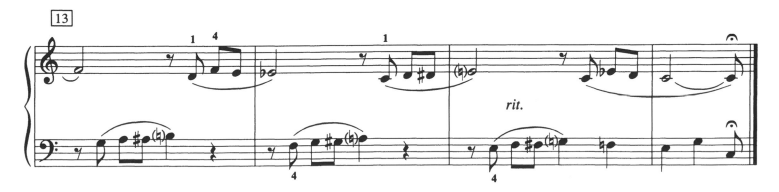